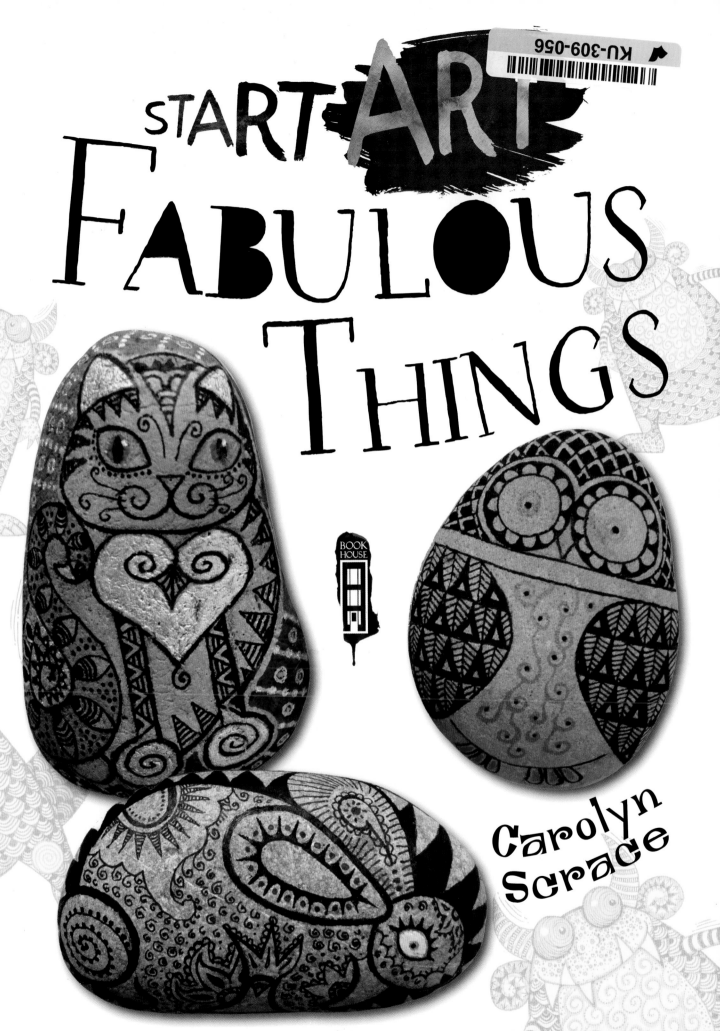

START ART

FABULOUS THINGS

BOOK HOUSE

Carolyn Scrace

Contents

Please note: sharp blades and scissors should be used under adult supervision.

Introduction

Discover the thrill of transforming mundane objects into exciting works of art! Have fun experimenting with different techniques and using a variety of materials to create works of art. Experimenting in this way develops drawing and design skills and encourages creativity.

Interesting objects

Keep a collection of interesting objects to draw on like stones, shells, drift wood, bottles, containers, old clothes and china. There are endless opportunities to embellish and decorate them.

Inspiration

Inspiration is all around you – even in the most surprising places! Carry a small sketchbook with you to capture any patterns and ideas. Stick in any magazine cuttings that inspire or excite you, and remember to use your sketch book as work in progress!

Creative confidence

As your creative confidence grows your skills and ability as an artist will increase too, enabling you to design and develop your own personal style of drawing.

Drawing on objects

Wherever you look there are objects simply waiting to be incorporated into artwork! Glass, cardboard, paper, fabric, stone, leaves and shells – the list of surfaces is endless. Drawing around three dimensional shapes, whether curved, flat, rounded or angular can be challenging – but the results are both exciting and surprising. Use this book as a springboard into the world of creating fabulous things!

Decorating leaves

Fallen leaves are great objects to decorate. Choose firm, waxy leaves with a simple shape. Experiment with different pens to find out which makes the best lines on the surface of the leaf. As a rule, white, gold and silver gel pens are best for drawing on dark colours and black fineliner pens are great for drawing on pale colours.

Decorating shells and pebbles

An abandoned snail shell is a terrifically inspiring shape to decorate. Use simple, bold patterns to follow the spiralling curve of the shell. Black fineliner and gold gel pens work well against this pale-coloured background.

See pages 10–11 to learn how to decorate pebbles.

Decorating cardboard tubes

A fantastic way to experiment with drawing on curved surfaces is to use the cardboard tube from a kitchen roll. Cut the tube in half and have fun trying out different patterns. Wacky faces make a fun theme to try first!

Pencil in the main shapes of the face. Go over the lines with black permanent marker pen. Block in areas of colour with felt-tips. Now start drawing patterns. Try white, silver and gold gel pens to draw on darker tones and black and dark-coloured gel pens on lighter areas.

Pencil sharpener

Eraser

Thick **marker pens** are perfect for filling in large areas. Fine **permanent marker** pens are great for outlines and details.

Graphite pencils come in different grades, from hard to soft.

Tools & materials

There are no special tools and materials needed for decorating fabulous things. A felt-tip pen and some old packaging is all you need to get started. You may, however, wish to use some or all of the tools and materials suggested here. It's important to experiment as some materials work better on certain surfaces than others.

Pencil crayons are ideal for adding soft shading to an area. Use them for colouring in.

Felt-tip pens come in a range of thicknesses. Thick pens are ideal for blocking-in large areas of colour.

Fineliner pens produce a flowing line and are ideal for intricate drawing. They come in a wide range of colours which creates added appeal.

A black gel pen is useful for outlines and detailed drawing. **Metallic and white gel pens** make the ideal choice for drawing onto darker colours.

Sequins

Double-sided tape

Sketchbook for jotting down ideas and trying out designs.

Use your sketchbook to experiment with new techniques and to keep notes of which materials were used.

Permanent fabric markers for drawing on cotton clothing. Air dry or iron to make the colours permanent.

Types of paper

Cartridge paper comes in a variety of thicknesses. Heavyweight paper is good for water-based paint. Note: ink lines may bleed (run) on some cartridge papers.

Bristol board or **paper** may be textured or smooth. Smooth Bristol board is good to work on with pencils, pencil crayons, markers, felt-tips and gel and fineliner pens for adding fine details.

Origami paper comes in a variety of thicknesses and finishes. Other types of paper (for example printing paper) can be used, provided it will fold and crease.

Palette (or clean saucer) for mixing paint.

Paintbrushes come in a wide range of sizes.

Coloured inks and **watercolour** paints are ideal for covering large areas of a design with subtle colour.

White acrylic primer is fast-drying and opaque. It produces a surface that is good for painting or drawing on.

Gouache is opaque watercolour. Use it for painting plain, flat areas.

Pebble animals

You will need:
Paper
Pebbles
Pencil
Fineliner pens
Gel pens

Smooth stones and pebbles are fantastic shapes to decorate. Try using the theme of animals to inspire your designs. Choose a selection of differently shaped stones to decorate.

1. Roughly sketch in the pebble outline then draw an animal inspired by its shape. Try adding some patterns.

2. Pencil the main shapes of your design onto the pebble.

3. Go over the pencil lines using a black fineliner and fine felt-tip pens.

4. Use white gel pen for the eye. Use delicate lines to add decorative patterns.

These cat and owl designs were used to decorate the pebbles shown opposite.

10

Use gold and silver gel pens to highlight areas such as the cat's ears, heart-shaped chest and paws.

See page 30 for a step-by-step guide to creating the feather pattern used to decorate the owl.

Using a bold, black zig-zag pattern around the edges makes the rabbit shape stand out.

11

Monster T-shirt!

Customise your T-shirt with a friendly monster!

1. Start by making a rough sketch of your design on scrap paper. **Artist's tip:** drawing the monster at an angle creates a more dynamic composition!

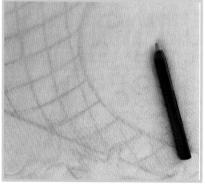

2. Trace the T-shirt shape onto A3 paper (or tape sheets together). Now pencil in your design and go over the lines with black felt-tip pen.

3. Cut out the paper shape and lay it inside the T-shirt on top of the cardboard. Use a yellow pencil crayon to trace the lines. Remove the paper.

4. Go over the lines with black fabric marker. Consider the tonal balance of your patterns; contrast pale yellow curls with dark black scales.

See page 30 for a guide to this scale pattern.

Artist's tip: use a limited palette of colours for a 'sophisticated' looking monster!

5. Follow the manufacturer's instructions to 'fix' the fabric marker pen lines.

13

Arty jars

Old jars are ready-made objects just waiting to be adorned with creative designs! Use them as personalised storage vessels or vases!

You will need:

Assorted, clean glass jars
Artist's white acrylic primer
Large paintbrush
Permanent markers
Metallic fine-pointed permanent markers
Paper kitchen towels
Raffia
Clear varnish (optional)

1. Protect your work surface with paper towels. Paint the outsides of the jars using acrylic primer and leave to dry.

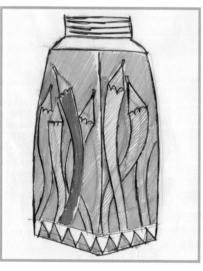

2. Make colour roughs of your ideas, using bold, simple designs.

3. Use black marker to draw in the main elements of the design. Start blocking in areas of colour.

4. Leave a thin white border round the main shapes then colour in the background. Add silver marker pen dots and a zig-zag border.

14

The design (below left) was inspired by a fairytale princess!

Experiment! Try leaving areas of clear glass when painting on primer. Then draw around the edges (see above).

Note: If permanent markers have been used, the finished designs can be coated with clear varnish.

5. As a finishing touch, wind raffia round the screw top, tie securely, then trim the ends.

Crazy collage

You will need:
Old magazines
Double-sided tape
Cartridge paper
Sequins
Buttons
Beads
Scissors
Felt-tip pens
Fineliner pens
PVA glue

A collage is a picture composed of different materials stuck down onto a background. This collage uses steampunk as its theme and combines magazine cuttings with drawings, sequins, buttons, beads and old keys!

1. Use magazine cuttings of faces and arms to stick onto cartridge paper (as shown). Draw in the shoulders.

2. Sketch in steampunk goggles, then complete the shape of the head with a series of drawings of cogs, wheels, nuts and bolts!

3. Draw in a huge moustache, a hat brim and a watch and chain. Block in areas with gold, grey and black felt-tips. Use fineliner pens for fine decoration.

4. Glue a selection of sequins, old buttons and beads onto your artwork. Old keys add an air of mystery to this collage.

Arty carton

Even the most ordinary carton or box can be transformed into a fabulous work of art!

You will need:
Cardboard carton
Tracing paper
Cartridge paper
Double-sided tape
Fineliner pens
Black marker pen
Scissors

1. Make thumbnail sketches of your ideas. This snake design winds around the carton.

2. Cut the tracing paper to wrap round the carton. Draw your design on it.

3. Trace your finished design onto cartridge paper and cut to fit. Tape it around the carton.

See page 30 for a guide to creating the pattern on the snake's body.

Artist's tip: highlight points of interest like a beetle, butterfly, flowers and the snake's head to ensure the design works from all viewpoints.

4. Now have fun decorating! Use black, white and grey decorations. Focus attention on specific areas by using spots of bright red pattern.

5. Add shading beneath the snake's body to make it stand out from the rest of the design.

Origami bird

You will need:
Square sheet of thin paper for folding

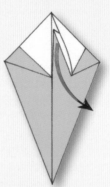

1. Fold in half, crease and unfold.

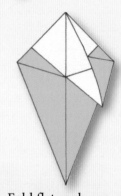
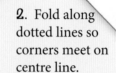

2. Fold along dotted lines so corners meet on centre line.

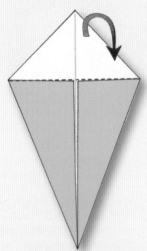

3. Fold top backwards along the dotted line.

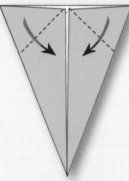

4. Fold inwards along the dotted line, then crease.

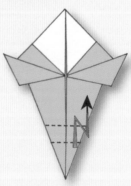

5. Pull inside outwards.

6. Fold flat as shown. Repeat on opposite side.

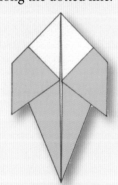

7. Repeat steps 5-6 on the other side.

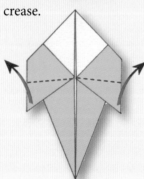

8. Fold upwards along the dotted lines.

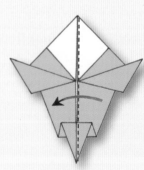

9. Make a zig-zag fold along the dotted lines, then crease.

10. Fold tail inwards, then crease.

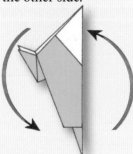

11. Turn sideways.

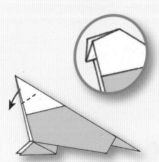

12. Make a pocket fold along the dotted line.

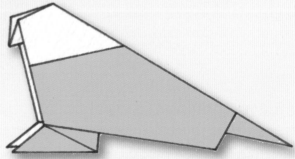

Now have fun creating!

Origami is the traditional Japanese art of folding squares of paper to create shapes representing animals and flowers.

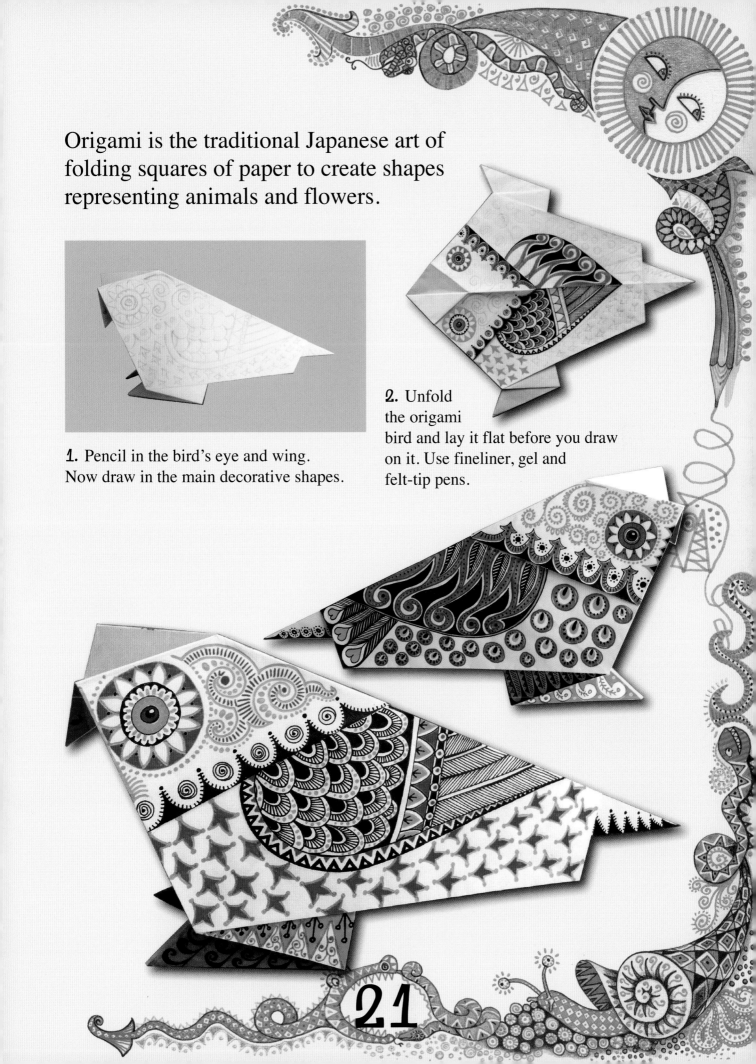

1. Pencil in the bird's eye and wing. Now draw in the main decorative shapes.

2. Unfold the origami bird and lay it flat before you draw on it. Use fineliner, gel and felt-tip pens.

Cupcakes

Fondant covered cupcakes are tremendous fun to draw on. Using the recipe (right), bake a tray of cupcakes in paper cases, then leave to cool. Note: ready made cupcakes are available in most supermarkets.

You will need:
Coloured fondant icing
    (or white fondant and
    food colouring)
Rolling pin
Sterilised lid
Sterilised pen top
Small kitchen knife
Edible ink felt-tip pens

Some adult supervision recommended.

Plain Vanilla Cupcakes

Ingredients
120g butter, softened
120g caster sugar
1 egg
1tsp vanilla extract
120g self-raising flour

Method
1. Preheat the oven to 180C/350F/Gas 4 and line a 12-hole muffin tin with paper cases.

2. Cream the butter and sugar together in a bowl until pale. Beat the eggs in a separate bowl and mix in along with the vanilla extract.

3. Fold in the flour, adding a little milk until the mixture is of a dropping consistency. Spoon the mixture into the paper cases until they are 1/4 full.

4. Bake in the oven for 10-15 minutes, or until golden-brown on top. Set aside to cool for 5-10 minutes. Then place on a wire rack.

1. Use a rolling pin to roll out some pale green fondant to about 3-4 mm (1/8th-3/16th inch). Use a sterilised plastic lid the same diameter as the top of the cupcakes to stamp out circular discs. Top the cakes with green, white or pink fondant.

2. Use a knife to cut squares out of the fondant trimmings. A sterilised pen top makes an ideal stamp for cutting out fondant spots. Arrange the squares and spots on top of the cupcakes, alternating the colours. Lightly dab the backs with water to stick them in place.

Cupcakes two

Simple patterns work best on fondant. Use green, pink and red coloured edible ink felt-tip pens to draw bold patterns.

Handy Hint

Keep scraps of left over rolled out icing. Use them for trying out your cake drawing materials. Note: most brands of edible ink felt-tip pens work best on dry icing.

1. Add edible ink felt-tip pen dots to the centres of the squares.

2. Draw petal shapes from each central dot to the four corners.

3. Draw dots in the centre of each white spot. Add six petal shapes.

4. Cover each tiny circle with dots. Draw six round petal shapes to form the flower.

5. Try to create as many different versions of these basic patterns as you can until you have decorated all the cupcakes.

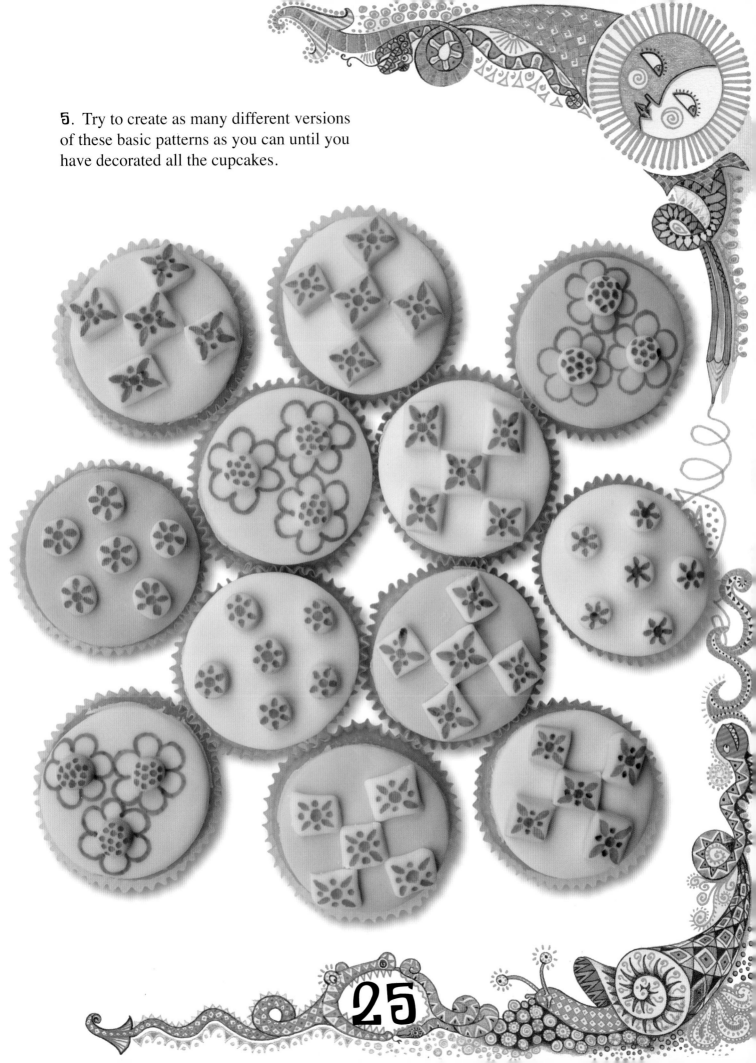

Glass and China

It is great fun and also very satisfying to decorate pieces of glass and china with patterns. Turn secondhand china and cheap or plain boring pieces into fantastic, personalised works of art!

Porcelain Pens

You can purchase pens to paint on porcelain from any good craft shop (most brands work on both china and glass). They are very easy to use. Simply draw your design, then let it air-dry. Some makes of pen need to be baked in a conventional oven to ensure the paint is dishwasher safe.

Handy Hint

Put a sheet of white paper inside clear glass to make it easier to see what your pattern looks like (above).

It is helpful to do rough drawings of the various designs you plan to use before starting work directly onto your china or glassware. Try to use designs that complement the shape or angles of the piece you are decorating.

Handy Hint

If your object needs to be baked, place it in a cold oven and let it heat up slowly. Allow to cool in the oven before removing.

Designer shoes

Make a bold fashion statement with your own unique designer shoes! All the shoes and boots shown here are made out of canvas. Draw on your designs using permanent fabric marker pens (available from all good craft shops).

1. Make a rough sketch of the shoes to try out your design ideas. Keep the main shapes of the design symmetrical. Shoes can have different patterns but they must look like a matching pair.

2. Remove the shoe laces, then begin drawing in the main shapes.

3. You may decide to leave parts of the shoes white (as above).

... and boots

Do you know how you want to decorate your boots? If not, make sketches of the boots to try out some designs before you start.

These boots proved ideal for a paisley-patterned design!

Pattern builder

These step-by-step examples show how to create some of the patterns used in this book.

Pebble animals... the owl (Pages 10-11)

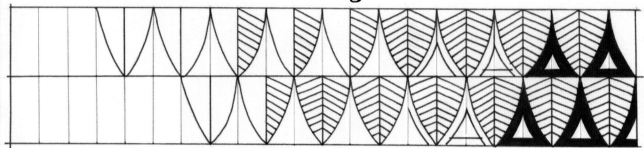

1. Ink in horizontal lines. Add vertical pencil guides. Ink in curved feather shapes (as shown).

2. Ink in a vertical line to represent the shaft of each feather and add rows of angled lines (as shown).

3. Add more curved lines to create thick borders and fill in with black fineliner.

Monster T-shirt (Pages 12-13)

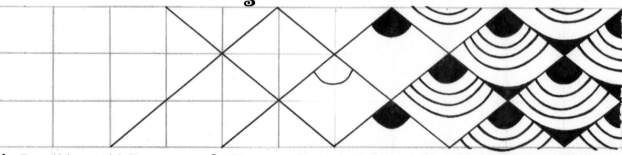

1. Pencil in a grid. Draw in diagonal lines in both directions (as shown).

2. Draw small semi-circles at the top of each diamond shape. Fill in as solid black.

3. Add small curved lines. Fill in the shape at the base of each diamond shape.

Arty carton... the snake (Pages 18-19)

1. Ink in horizontal lines. Draw two zig-zag lines and fill with circles (as shown).

2. Draw smaller versions above. Fill the lower triangles with alternating angled lines.

3. Fill the base with short vertical lines to represent the snake's underbelly.

Glossary

Background area behind an object or image.

Blocking in where areas of flat colour are put down.

Collage a technique for making a work of art by sticking pieces of different materials like paper, cloth, or wood onto a flat surface.

Colour rough a quick sketch of the principle coloured elements in a picture.

Composition how an artist arranges shapes, sizes and colours, the different elements that make a piece of art.

Customise to modify or change the appearance of an item to suit an individual.

Design a graphic representation, usually a drawing or a sketch.

Dynamic concerned with energy or motion.

Embellish to improve or make beautiful by adding detail or ornament.

Intensity a measurement of difference between a colour and pure grey.

Layout an arrangement, plan, or design.

Limited palette when an artist restricts the number of colours used.

Origami the Japanese art, or process, of folding paper into recognisable shapes.

Raffia a fibre used for tying, weaving etc.

Rough a quick sketch of the main elements in a picture.

Sequins a small piece of shiny metal foil or plastic used to decorate fabric.

Sketch a preparatory drawing.

Steampunk a type of fantasy art, featuring machines and other technology, based on steam power of the 19th century.

Technique an accepted method used to produce something.

Three dimensions having, or appearing to have, the dimension of depth as well as width and height.

Thumbnail (sketches) usually small, quick, abbreviated drawings.

31

Index